MEGA BUTTOCKS AND LEGS

Scientific Buttocks and Legs Training

Iván Salinas Román

Mega Buttocks and Legs
Kindle Direct Publishing
Paperback edition 2021

Dedicated for those who think that ... if you are not going to take care of your body, then where do you plan to live?

CONTENTS

FOREWORD

The glute and the legs, whether you are a woman or a man, are without a doubt the two largest and most powerful muscle groups in the body, which obviously look great when they are well worked. However, the legs and buttocks are muscle groups that many people find difficult to develop for most people.

The glutes control a large number of athletic movements, helping you lift more weight, progress in other exercises, but also jump higher and run faster.

If we develop the glutes well, we can improve the transfer of force to the rest of the body so that we can lift more and not injure them. In addition to that if you like to preach high mobility sports it will help you improve in matters of acceleration speed, vertical jump and changes of directions. Gluteal training is something very interesting to analyze, since many studies and most important research on the training of this large muscle group are still not well known in most athletes, hence the understanding of the way in which we have have to be trained, which is why most people's glutes are very weak compared to how strong, large, and powerful they could become with proper training.

Now, leg training has been underrated by men and overrated by women, and it is no coincidence that men are the ones who complain the most that their legs do not grow as they would like. Some people tend to blame their genetics and although genetics play an important role when it comes to developing any muscle group, it should be noted that when you have smart training, the right nutrition and adequate rest, you can achieve great results.

To maximize and take your legs to the next level in this you will learn how to perform an intelligent and correct leg training, based on scientific evidence, so that you develop your entire lower body in a timely manner, both your legs, glutes, hamstrings (hamstrings) and calves.

You will understand both the benefits and the errors when training the leg, you will understand the best exercises for your training, the technique when executing them with images and the muscles involved.

On the other hand, the glutes, unfortunately, this great musculature remains asleep almost all day in most of the people. Its main function seems to be to cushion our long hours sitting. Modern life damages its aesthetics and inhibits its function.

The gluteus is a muscle group with three main protagonists: the gluteus maximus, the gluteus medius and the gluteus minimus.

The gluteus maximus (or maximum) is the largest and most superficial muscle, representing 2/3 of the total size. It is a powerful hip extender (pushes it forward). Therefore, it helps to straighten your body in the rise of movements such as deadlifts or squats.

The gluteus medius, together with the gluteus medius, rotates the hip outward and abducts the leg (separates it from the body). Gluteus medius weakness often leads to poor stability and more lower back pain.

In this book regarding the buttocks, you will learn to carry out a science-based training, to fully exploit its development, you will learn the techniques of the best exercises with images, you will get tips and guidelines to take your buttocks to the next level.

I am going to share with you, whether you are a man or a woman, regardless of whatever your training level is, what exercises you have to do, what tricks you can apply, how to manage loads, how to train intensity, frequency, series, breaks, etc.

Benefits of training legs

Correctly training your legs is important for many aspects, beyond the aesthetic. I will tell you about some benefits:

Lose more fat

Training large muscles involves investing a greater number of calories and multi-joint exercises involve a greater number of muscles, which also leads to a higher caloric expenditure.

In leg workouts it is necessary to include several multi-joint exercises that affect large muscles, which leads us to training legs to burn or oxidize more calories than to train some other muscles or smaller muscle groups.

Strengthen the lumbar

The lumbar is an area of our body that must support, for much of the day, the weight of our torso.

The lumbar are part of the core, or center of the body, an area in charge of fulfilling important functions, including stabilizing ourselves in different movements and actions.

In many of the leg exercises, such as squats, deadlifts or lunges, the action of the lumbar will be necessary to help stabilization, which means working and strengthening them in each session.

A strong lumbar will better support that constant load that the weight of our torso supposes, and can be the solution to many aches and pains in it.

Transfer and improvement in other sports

Leg training moves beyond the activity in the gym, since the legs in many sports are the main component that makes the effort, or intervenes in a remarkable and totally necessary way.
Running, soccer, walking, hiking, cycling, swimming, basketball and so on. That is why the importance of training the legs at a sports level.

Increasing strength, endurance, strengthening joints, or improving certain movements will be some of the advantages that we will obtain by training the leg and that we can transfer to any sport that we practice outside the gym.

It allows us to improve aesthetics

This is obvious, but one of the most unsightly things that we can find in a gym body is the fact of having a great volume imbalance between torso and legs.

So there is no excuse not to train and gain volume in legs.

Testosterone boost

Bodybuilding training is directly linked to testosterone production. This is because when we perform multi-joint exercises (especially those known as basic), the male body is forced to generate testosterone.

Within these basic multi-joint exercises we find a couple that involve the use of the legs:

➢ Squats
➢ The dead weight

Testosterone is an essential hormone for muscle growth to occur, a goal sought by many of those who skip leg training with some assiduity.

In the case of women, it helps to improve the general condition of the hips and buttocks, as it improves blood circulation, preventing the formation of fat nodules and fluid retention that cause disorders such as cellulite.

Benefits of training glutes

Improve posture

A consequence of "sitting sickness", both men and women suffer from poor posture. Tight and shortened hip flexors, weak and overstretched hip extensors, and glutes that "forget" how to properly activate all contribute to the most commonly observed postural deviation: backswing and kyphosis-lordosis.
In addition, leaning forward at the hips pushes the abdomen outward, creating the illusion of a tummy even in the absence of excess abdominal fat.

Pain reduction and injury prevention

Strong glutes support the lower back, but when the glutes are not strong enough to perform their hip extension function, the muscles that were not designed for this work will.

Over time, these "helper" muscles can overexert themselves, resulting in pain and compression of the lumbar spine, hips, and knees.

Better athletic performance

The gluteus maximus is capable of generating an enormous amount of power. This power can be translated into sport-specific speed, acceleration, vertical distance, and endurance.

Training your glutes can powerfully assist you in various athletic gestures, propelling your body forward and improving your running, jumping, and cycling faster, stronger, and longer.

Try adding a day or two of strength training to your lower body on days when you don't plan on going out for a long run or riding your bike.

Increased bone density

Bone density peaks sometime between 5 to 10 years after we have reached skeletal maturity.

Beginning at the young age of 30, old, damaged bone is reabsorbed faster than new bone formation, resulting in an increased risk of osteopenia (less than normal bone density) and osteoporosis (a progressive disease of the bones). bones).

Exercises that place mechanical stress on the bones, including lower-bone weight training, running, and some forms of yoga, can postpone and even reverse the effects of age-related loss of bone density.

The earlier you start incorporating them into your training, the greater their potential benefits.

Loss of fat

Fat loss requires a daily caloric deficit. Burn more calories than you consume and you will lose fat (more or less).

Unlike adipose tissue, muscle is metabolically active, meaning that even if you are not exercising, your muscles will burn calories from stored fat.

Since the glutes and hamstrings are two of the largest muscle groups in the body, their potential contribution to fat loss cannot be overstated.

Best Leg Exercises

One more reason to include leg training is the number of muscles that are part of it:

> - Quadriceps
> - Hamstrings
> - Buttocks
> - Solo
> - Twins
> - Abductors

The first thing that is key and remember is, which are the muscles involved in training, so it is important to understand that not all leg exercises work the muscle groups equally, in this book I will explain in detail all the exercises to legs, but we are going to start a base of exercises, so that you can start from there.

So I'm going to show you to start, the 3 exercises that with scientific foundations that you should include in your leg routine, to be able to provide the greatest activation to these muscle groups, without the need to add so many isolation or machine exercises, if you want a short and effective routine.

As I mentioned this would be the base, from there you would start to add other isolation exercises or machines.

1.-Squat and its variants

It is obvious that this exercise would be, since it is a multi-joint exercise that is proven to use up to 200 muscles when performing its execution. Later I will explain the technique, benefits and muscles involved when performing.

2.- Hip Thrust

When it comes to developing and achieving large and strong glutes, there is no more effective exercise than the Hip thrust, since it is the one that generates the most activation in this muscle group. Later I will explain the technique, benefits and muscles involved when executing.

3.-Deadlift and its variants

The hamstrings are one of the most forgotten groups, for something they are the muscles that are injured the most, so you have to give them their place in training apart from that they give you very good volume to the leg and what better than one of the best exercises that we can perform with weights the deadlift and its variants. Later I will explain the technique, benefits and muscles involved when executing.

The best glute exercises

The glutes are versatile muscles, involved in a multitude of movements. Therefore, the best way to train them is by incorporating different planes and angles, also varying the volume and intensity of the exercises.

In addition, different movements involve to a greater or lesser extent different portions of each of the muscles that make up the buttocks, achieving a greater stimulus thanks to a good combination.

Therefore, we must not neglect the basic principles of training. At the base must always be the great movements, which in this case will be 3: Hip thrust, Squat and its variants, the deadlift and its variants.
Also, we must integrate assistance work, without forgetting the lateral exercises that involve the gluteus medius to a greater extent, like all those in charge of abducting the hip.

Likewise, we must add a certain variety of isolation exercises with less intensity will achieve a good additional stimulus, improving the results. Isolation exercises are also useful to correct possible muscular imbalances between sides.

Taking all this into account the best gluteal exercises are:

> - ➤ Hip thrust
> - ➤ Glute bridge or gluteal bridge
> - ➤ Pull through
> - ➤ Sumo Squat
> - ➤ Deadlift and its variants
> - ➤ Lunges or strides
> - ➤ Bulgarian squat
> - ➤ Step-up

I am going to detail all these exercises so that you can do them with the correct technique and get the most out of it.

Glute Workout Vectors - Horizontal and Vertical

To understand glute training and get it fully developed first of all we have to understand that there are three main movement patterns that activate the glutes.

The movements with vertical force vectors such as:

> ➢ Squat and its variants
> ➢ Deadlift and its variants
> ➢ Strides
> ➢ Bulgarian squat

The movements with horizontal force vectors such as:

> ➢ Hip thrust
> ➢ Glute bridge or gluteal bridge
> ➢ Pull through

The problem is that most people train almost pure vertical force vector exercises like squats and deadlifts, adding a few combined force vector exercises like lunges, horizontal force vector movements have been shown to activate much more. the glutes that we analyze vertically the most important movements with a vertical force vector.

TRAINING VARIABLES

The training variables are the components that every training plan includes and that must be considered to obtain the expected results. These variables are the intensity of the effort, the volume of training, the frequency of training, the rest between repetitions, series and exercises; the order and selection of exercises and the cadence or speed of execution. We will mainly talk about the volume, intensity and frequency of training.

What is training volume?

When we talk about volume, we are basically talking about the total amount of work done for a given period of time. We can talk about weekly volume or volume per training session and we will be referring to the number of repetitions by the number of series performed during that period.

Volume is a fundamental variable in both hypertrophy and strength. In the latter, it is usually a matter of bringing a lower volume and raising other variables such as intensity, which we will talk about below. On the other hand, in hypertrophy, a higher volume is usually chosen.

Training volume is the total number of sets and reps in a workout. It is one of the most important variables when it comes to quantifying and scheduling training, progression and gains in muscle mass will depend on performing a good volume of training. Starting by calculating and meeting the minimum effective volume.

What is training intensity?

If we talk about intensity we are talking about the weight used, the breaks or the speed, if we talk about cardiovascular exercise. The shorter the rest time, the greater the intensity and, conversely, the lower the weights used, the lower the intensity.

This is also essential to achieve our goals and, normally, in a hypertrophy training we speak of a medium intensity while in a strength training the intensity is maximum. In conventional, long-duration cardio, we speak of medium intensity while in HIIT we speak of high intensity. These are just a few examples to put us in the situation.

Intensity is an important training variable, often misunderstood. Many people in the gym think that they train at a good intensity when in reality it is not even 60% of what you can give and you are not progressing. It is essential to perform series with a high intensity and degree of effort, otherwise the series will not work and you will never progress.

Many define intensity based on subjective sensations, such as how tired they have left the gym or the stiffness they feel in the following days. However, from an objective point of view intensity can refer to the intensity of the load or the intensity of the effort; how much weight you are lifting (usually referred to a specific RM or percentage of 1RM) or how close that load is to your maximum effort (usually defined as a scale value of perceived exertion or RPE, for the acronym in English of " Rating of Perceived Exertion "), respectively.

Currently, a new way of measuring intensity in training has been evidenced, such as the RIR. They are the repetitions in the bedroom or the ones you have left until you reach muscle failure. Experts and studies tell us that it is more effective to take into account those repetitions that you have left until you reach failure than to constantly reach failure. So that you understand, I will give you a simple example.

If for a training series you have stipulated to perform 12 repetitions, the ideal intensity to gain muscle mass should be RIR2-3, this means 2-3 repetitions before failing. So if for that set of 12, I roughly calculate the load that I can tolerate up to 12, and you perform 9 or 10, it will be more effective than failing at rep 12.

Hence, the intensity has to be high, you have to put a load that you can not do more than 12 repetitions, but instead of 12, you do 10. And with that you will progress a lot.

What is the frequency of training?

When talking about frequency, we are basically talking about how many times we work the same muscle group in a period of time, usually a week. We speak of frequency one if we work each muscle group once a week or frequency three, for example, if we train each muscle three times a week.

Normally, frequency one is associated with weider type workouts and frequency two and three with torso-leg or full-body workouts, although this does not always have to be the case.

The frequency of training understood as the number of times we execute a pattern or muscle group per week.

The training frequency has to be measured by intensity and volume, because the greater the volume within the session, the less training frequency you will give per week. And vice versa.

It has been seen that there may be slight improvements in training from frequency 2, that is, repeating a muscle group twice a week, but, nevertheless, it is not so decisive if we keep everything well adjusted. This works like clockwork. If you have well adjusted the weekly volume and intensity, no matter how much you touch it once a week, you will also progress.

HYPERTROPHY: METABOLIC STRESS AND MECHANICAL TENSION

Hypertrophy: mechanisms to stimulate it

Scientific evidence shows that there are two ways to stimulate hypertrophy: mechanical stress and metabolic stress. It is interesting to recognize each of them, their characteristics and see which one interests us most in order to produce hypertrophy. 3 elements are required to create hypertrophy: mechanical tension, muscle stress and muscle laceration or damage, to which many authors also agree in adding the time under tension, that is, the duration of the exercises. Mechanical stress and metabolic stress work by producing muscle damage. Repairing that muscle damage, adding the supercompensation principle, will lead to a greater amount of resulting muscle mass (you know, if eating and resting are adequate according to a well-structured work plan).

Mechanical stress

It is the most important element to produce hypertrophy. That is, when new muscle tissue is produced, the highest percentage has been due to applied mechanical stress. Mechanical or muscular tension, in turn, is obtained by playing with two factors:

➤ Intensity: that is, the weight of the loads.

➤ Duration, or what is the same, the time the muscle remains under tension.

Why do we say that it is the most decisive? Well, because the evidence tells us that, if we play with these two components, maintaining during intense periods (with high loads) of 40 to 50 seconds per series, a mechanical tension on a muscle, we are going to recruit or activate the greatest number of motor units or fibers. That is, we are going to break more fibers, therefore, more fibers to repair, more supercompensation, more new fibers = hypertrophy.

Metabolic stress

The metabolic stress resulting from exercise can provide a valuable hypertrophy stimulus. It works from a metabolic route (or way of obtaining energy) anaerobic, that is, in the absence of oxygen. Energy for muscle contractions from exercise is derived from glucose. This process is called anaerobic glycolysis. The speed at which you need glucose energy in this type of training is higher than the speed with which we are able to oxidize the glucose molecule from oxygen, which is why it is anaerobic. But this process leaves a lot of METABOLIC GARBAGE behind. Lactate mainly and also hydrogen and phosphorus.

This accumulation of metabolic waste produces metabolic alterations, at a chemical level in our body, which promote the anabolic hormonal environment, that is, the creation of muscle tissue. For this accumulation of metabolites to be greater, they work in sessions with shorter rest times between series (30 seconds - 1 minute). This is done so that there is no time to recover the phosphagen completely (it takes 2 to 3 minutes if the previous series was executed correctly) and each time there is a higher waste saturation which will lead to fatigue.

If you are looking for new muscle tissue, hypertrophy, where are you going to get it from: Training, eating in caloric surplus and rest. Within the training, you need yes or yes to cause muscle damage. You can already be years in the gym that, if you do not produce muscle damage, you will not gain more muscle.

Sets, reps, and breaks

Repetitions are understood as the number of times in a row that the same movement is repeated. The series (or batches) group a certain number of repetitions, separated by periods of rest or by the performance of different exercises. A session corresponds to the set of series - usually of different movements - that are carried out in a row. For example, a session can group 6 different exercises, of each of which do 4 sets with 15 repetitions in each of them.

The number of repetitions and sets, as well as the rest period between them can vary depending on the specific goals. How to gain strength, muscle mass or endurance.

• To gain strength: few repetitions (3-5) with high loads (> 85% of your 1RM. 1RM = maximum weight you can lift one time).

• To develop muscular endurance: high repetitions (> 15-20) with low loads (<60% of your 1RM).

• To promote hypertrophy: we stay in the middle, hence the classic 8-12 reps with intermediate loads (60-85% of your 1RM).

Note that there is no rep range to tone or define. The only thing you can do is gain muscle and lose fat. If your coach proposes you to define with some rep range, serious advice is looking for another.

The principle of specificity is valid, but flexible. You can gain strength and muscle in a wide range of repetitions. Training to failure with the big moves is not recommended (especially in novices). Adding it from time to time in less demanding exercises can contribute to total hypertrophy (increased metabolic stress).

Progress is the only way to hypertrophy. If you increase the weights gradually the muscles will grow. Progressing can also mean doing some extra repetition with the same weight.

Periodizing is the only way to make long-term progress and break deadlocks. As you progress, your work capacity increases, and you need to add more volume in a smart way.

To achieve a global fitness you must work different ranges of repetitions. Strength is essential, but you also need a minimum of muscular endurance.

How much do you have to rest between sets?

It is one of the big questions when it comes to training in the gym, knowing the exact time we should rest between sets to gain muscle mass or strength.

If you are training to gain strength (1-5 reps), it is recommended to rest for 3-5 minutes between sets.

If, on the other hand, you are training to gain muscle mass, in a wider range of repetitions (6-20), it is recommended to rest between 1 minute and a minute and a half.

I think going by the clock to determine your recovery is a big mistake and I'm going to explain why.

It is true that for certain sports the watch is decisive. For example, if you are doing a functional training to improve in boxing, in that case, the duration of the rounds and the rest times between rounds are already predefined by the sport, so it is logical to work according to those rest times. that boxing imposes on you.

However, to train solely to improve your physique, I do not see any sense since the rest needs will be closely linked to your physical condition.

Heating or Activation

When we talk about warming up or activating ourselves before starting our weight routine, we have to differentiate a warm-up from a stretch. And that stretching before is not interesting, because it can not hurt. The interesting thing is to carry out series of approximations, it prepares our body for the activity that we are going to carry out.

In a stretch, the muscle fibers will stretch, the reality is that the muscles will begin to elongate, it will have flexibility and if you are going to do some type of training either in the weight room or when running a marathon or playing games. A soccer match is not going to suit you so much, because for this activity you need the greatest contraction of your muscle fibers, you need the muscle to be ready and powerful to be able to do the contractions and if you stretch before your activity the Muscle will not be able to contract 100% therefore, physical activity and your performance will decrease significantly.

You will wonder then what should I do before entering a game or what should I be before entering the weight room, because the answer is in the warm-ups. And what is a warm-up? They are basically mobilizations, it is moving the parts of your body that are going to be used when performing your physical activity, but they should not be crazy movements, they should be movements that simulate the physical activity that you are going to perform. For example, if you are going to run 100 meters, you can do a sprint, this should not be so strong, I finish mildso that you give the information to your brain that those muscles are the ones that have to be activated in the future and thus are well coordinated as a good teamwork.

Another example if you are going to load 200 kilos in free squat, a perfect warm-up is to squat with your own weight or only with the bar and thus, little by little you will increase the weight until you reach 200 kg, this is called a prisoner approach.

Since you are preparing the brain to say these muscles are the ones that are going to have to activate when you squat with greater weight and thus avoid injuries. the response mobilizations or warming.

A classic error in warm-ups is when you go to work for example shoulder or arm and they send you to warm up on the treadmill or on the bicycle there it does not make sense because in reality you are sending the information to your brain, that the muscles that are It has to be activated in the future because it will be the legs when you are going to train the upper part, there is a mistake.

Stretching can help and can be very useful, but these should be used after the activity, after your game because when doing this type of activity and depending on the intensity in which you do it, the muscles will find very, very tense after any physical activity.

All that tension will be reduced, it will be eliminated little by little if we stretch, remember especially for people who are in the weight room, it is good to be strong, it is good to be strong, but if you can combine it with flexibility. that they are going to give you the stretches because you are going to do the perfect combination between strength and flexibility and therefore it will be very difficult for you to injure yourself in any other physical activity that is why stretching is important.

GLUTEO ACTIVATION OR WARM UP

Stride stretch: 15 seconds duration each leg.

Monsters Walks: 15 steps to both sides, 2 times.

Back kick: 12 reps with each leg. 2 times

Glute Bridge: 20 repetitions.

STRENGTH TRAINING

Normally we talk about strength routines and hypertrophy routines, they are routines with different objectives, but we really don't know how they differ. What makes a routine to be hypertrophy or strength?

The objective is different and the structure is also completely different, the training and rest days are different and there are even exercises that differ and that usually only go in one type of routine

Strength

When performing strength routines, as the name suggests, the main objective is to increase the strength of our muscles. This type of gain can be applied in many areas since a gain in strength implies an increase in power, running speed, delays muscle fatigue, etc. Training a strength routine means lifting loads close to 100% of 1RM (Repetition Maximum). This means that we will be working almost to the best of our ability.

In this way, when we are immersed in a routine to gain strength we must perform between 5 and 8 sets with each exercise. Each of them will consist of between 1 and 6 repetitions. Likewise, it is convenient to perform exercises that involve several muscle groups at the same time. We talk about exercises such as squats, hip thrust, shoulder press, bench press or deadlift.

HIP THRUST: Technique and muscles involved

The hip thrust is one of the most used exercises to work the lower body due to the activation of the muscles involved in the movement. It is used for different objectives: improving sports performance, injury rehabilitation, hypertrophy etc.

The hip thrust is a hip dominant exercise, one of the main movement patterns of the human body. It is a global and multi-joint exercise that activates large muscle groups in movement.

There are exercises that favor the gluteal muscles such as lunges, squats, etc., but they are not enough. The largest muscle group in the human body is the buttocks, therefore, they need an exercise that isolates them and works them intensively. The best exercise for glutes is the hip thrust, by far it is the one that activates the glute the most.

MUSCLES INVOLVED

THE HIP THRUST is a multi-joint exercise involving many muscle groups.

The muscles involved in this exercise are mainly:

• The primary extensors of the hip (gluteus maximus. It is where it is most activated, hamstrings and some fibers of the adductor magnus).

• The secondary extensors of the hip (adductors and posterior fibers of the gluteus medius and gluteus minimus).

• Spinal stabilizers (spinal erectors)

• The flexor-extensors of the knee (rectus femoris and vastus).

TECHNIQUE

Initial position

• The initial position of the person is sitting on the floor and with the upper part of the back supported by a padded bench or box.

• If the exercise is performed with a bar loaded with discs, the performer will have to roll the bar over the legs to the hips.

• The feet are placed at the width of the hips or shoulders and with the knees bent around 90º.

• It is recommended to place a padding on the bar for heavy lifting to avoid discomfort in the hip bones.

Hip thrust (concentric phase)

• Raise the buttocks off the floor by doing a

• hip extension keeping the contact points of the feet on the ground and the scapular area on the bench.

• The head and spine must remain in a neutral position throughout the movement.

• The hip extension is performed until the body reaches a position parallel to the ground. The idea is to be in that position for two seconds and return to the starting position.

DEADLIFT AND ITS VARIANTS

One of the most complete exercises that we can perform is the deadlift in any of its variants. Despite the fact that many call it an exercise "with a high risk of injury", performed with correct technique does not have to give us any problems and its benefits are numerous.

The deadlift is one of the basic and main exercises of any strength training routine, whatever the sports specialty. His technique is not as simple as it may seem since the simultaneity required in hip extension and knee extension needs his learning.

Stability is essential in the deadlift, which is why it is recommended to work with flat shoes or barefoot.

When performing deadlifts we have different variants that help us to enhance the work of certain muscle groups. They are all multi-joint and very functional exercises, but we can combine the different variants depending on the needs and objectives of our training. Among the most popular deadlifts are conventional deadlifts, sumo, stiff legs, and hexagonal deadlifts.

Conventional or traditional deadlift: Technique and muscles involved

The basic one, that of a lifetime. It is the most common, it is a movement that can generate force in the real world and burn many calories, while developing the muscles of the back, arms and thighs and also provides great stability of the trunk. If you're serious about your fitness, you'll want to integrate deadlifts into your training.

Technique

- The bar must be glued to the tibias.

- The weight should be on the heels.

- You have to follow this order: head, hip, knee and ankle. It is common to make mistakes such as putting the hips below the knees or the head below the hips.

- Activate the glutes and dynamically stretch the piriformis and hip flexors before performing the movement.

- The back must be completely straight with the gluteus back and the hips engaged, keeping tension on the spine.

- Push your chest out and tuck your scapulae back.

Muscles involved

• Lumbar muscles (quadratus lumbar).
• Hips (buttocks).
• Femoral (hamstring) muscles.
• Quadriceps (thighs).
• Dorsal muscles.
• Forearms.
• Trapezoids.

These are the muscles involved when performing a single exercise ... as you will see it is great for gaining strength and muscle mass!

For this reason it is often said that the conventional deadlift is the most recommended functional exercise of all bodybuilding.

SUMO DEADLIFT: Technique and muscles involved

The sumo deadlift is one of the most common variants of the deadlift and in fact it is accepted in powerlifting, depending on our levers and our objective we will decide if we do one or the other or what days to allocate them for each one.

Técnica

In this variant of the deadlift, the arms are positioned inside the legs. The width of the leg opening will largely depend on the flexibility of each lifter.

It is important to adopt a position where the tibiae are perpendicular to the ground, in this way the force exerted by the legs will be more effective.

The shins should be positioned a couple of centimeters away from the bar before grabbing it. If you start with the shinbones glued to the bar, once you squat down you will shift the weight and with it the starting position.

The knees should point outward and the feet should turn slightly outward so that the toes are in line with the knees. Make sure your feet are firm on the platform.

The next step is to bend over and grab the bar. The arms should be straight and inside the legs. Your grip is likely somewhere between the rough and ready part of the bar. Don't worry, with the help of magnesium, your grip shouldn't fail.

Position the scapulae on the bar, this would be the ideal position to lift the weight in a straight line.

Keep your hips low and your back flat, almost straight. You should not look down or up. Look at an imaginary point about six feet away on the ground.

In sumo deadlift, take-off is slower and more complicated. Once the weight is off the ground, build momentum and push the ground down with your legs. The bar should rise in a straight line to the locked position.

Since the back is held almost straight from the start of the lift, most of the work is done with the legs and traps.

The slow, controlled pull at the start is the most important. Don't rush or do an aggressive pull. Make sure your arms are straight, don't bend them.

DEADLIFT SEMI-DIRECTED OR ROMANIAN LEGS: Technique and muscles involved

Of these two ways of calling the Romanian deadlift, the one that would be technically more correct is the semi-rigid leg deadlift since during the Romanian deadlift the knees must be slightly flexed.

The Romanian deadlift is one of the best exercises you can do to develop the posterior chain (hamstrings, glutes, and back). It's easy to learn, load, and program, and when done right, it's perfectly safe too.

What muscles does the Romanian deadlift work?

The Romanian deadlift is one of the most effective exercises for glute and hamstring strengthening. In addition, it is one of the best allies to strengthen the lower back and all the muscles that maintain the spine, which improves body posture and balance.

TECHNIQUE

• The movement starts from the top, holding the bar at shoulder width or slightly higher.

• Feet at the width of the hips and points to the front.

• Head relaxed, chest up and just at the beginning of the movement the knees at 15º-20º of flexion.

• The movement begins by pushing the hips back as the bar travels down our thighs to just below the kneecaps approximately. During the movement we remember to maintain the alignment of our spine, maintaining lordosis and natural kyphosis in the lumbar and cervical spine respectively.

• At this point we will notice the stretch in our hamstrings and we will begin to extend our hips as the bar rises in contact with our thighs.

• By fully extending the hips and returning to our starting position, we strongly contract the glutes.

SQUAT: Technique and muscles involved

Squats are the basis of many training plans, so it is important to know how to perform them well. This exercise focuses on the thighs (quads and hamstrings) and glutes, but also works on core strength and stability.

Technique

Get into a position that is comfortable for you: Some people find it helpful to put their toes out. It begins standing up, looking straight ahead and with a straight back. We must put our hands on the bar and push our shoulders back to maintain a correct lumbar posture, while the feet are separated from the width of the shoulders. The bar used should be placed just above the traps, it should not rest on the neck.

A.   **B.**

MUSCLES INVOLVED

Quadriceps:

It is the main muscle most involved in squats. Having good quadriceps is very important for anyone, since with it we can stretch our legs, elevate our body and lift and move our body mass, all of them functions that we perform on a daily basis. If your sport is running, cycling or triathlon, you will know how important it is to have strong legs, so if you are not doing squats yet, start including them in your workouts.

Glutes and hamstrings:

Without these muscles, our torso could not stand upright. With squats we can reinforce this very important muscle group in anyone who practices sports. Having glutes and hamstrings in good condition can make a difference at the end of a race where fatigue begins to take its toll.

Abs and lower back (Erector spinal):

Having a strong torso is the foundation of every athlete. It helps us maintain a good body posture, thus avoiding lumbar problems, we gain stability and balance, and it helps us keep the spine stabilized during training. When we squat, these muscle groups are also involved, if it weren't for them our spine and neck would go forward losing stability, so it is of special attention to have a worked torso to avoid all kinds of pain and / or injuries.

Twins:

They are the muscles that are probably least involved in squatting, but they are required to prevent our legs from moving forward during the exercise.

SUMO SQUAT

You already know that squats are a very popular option in lower body training, where there are several protagonists involved: the entire leg, the lower back and the gluteus. But do all squats work the glute the same way? What is more effective: go down a lot or not go down so much? Does the separation between the feet affect anything?

The classic squat is not the best for the glute. The most efficient option would be the so-called sumo squat or squat with legs spread with the balls of the feet pointed more outward than usual. A position that affects the muscles of the inner thigh to a greater extent.

TECHNIQUE

1. Spread your legs so that your heels are at a similar distance from shoulder to shoulder and point your feet outward. Imagining a clock and striking ten to two is a good trick.

2. Lower yourself until your hips are on the same line, at the same height as your knees, or lower as far as you can. As there is a lot of muscle involved more actively, you will feel that going down and going up is easier, costing less than in the classic squat.

3. Therefore, to really take advantage of your training time, you must do the sumo squat with weight.

BULGARIAN SQUAT

The Bulgarian squat is one of those exercises that cannot be missed in a medium / advanced routine that seeks a good result at the lower body level, especially in gluteal hypertrophy.

When performing the Bulgarian squat, as with most exercises, correct positioning is key. The closer together your legs are, the more you target your quads. The further you move the front leg in front of you off the bench, the more emphasis you put on your glutes.

The Bulgarian squats:

• They give a better range of motion
• They overload the quadriceps and glutes, affecting each one more or less depending on the position.
• Recruit your stabilizing muscles
• They develop strength in the core muscles
• Improves balance and strength in the muscles around the knee
• Reduces muscle imbalance by working unilaterally.
• Allows variety in weights and locations, both for the material we use as support and for

the one we use to get the ballast (dumbbells, bars, kettlebell, buckets ...)

• Makes squat days more varied and fun

LUNGES: Technique and muscles involved

Many people often overlook the benefits of unilateral (single leg) exercises when designing a leg routine and focus their workouts on exercises such as squats and deadlifts, neglecting exercises such as lunges.

Unilateral exercises can help compensate for any type of muscle or strength decompensation between each side of the body, as well as improve strength in other heavier compound exercises, because unilateral exercises correct weaknesses in the synergistic muscles (muscles smaller than help stabilize the joint).

The stride is an exercise mainly designed to work the lower body, especially requesting the legs and buttocks. Of the leg muscles, the thigh or quadriceps are mainly worked and if the stride is wider, the hamstrings and gluteus are also applied.

MUSCLES INVOLVED

The primary muscles that are worked with the stride are:

• the gluteus maximus muscle

• the quadriceps (quadriceps femoris muscle)

The secondary muscles that are worked are:

• the biceps femoris muscle (or biceps femoris),

• the semimembranosus muscle

• the semitendinosus muscle and calf muscles

TECHNIQUE

1. Step forward with your left leg and lower your right knee slowly toward the ground. The tip of the left foot should point forward, the hips down, and the leading knee should not go beyond the ankle.

2. Stop the movement when your left knee is at an angle of about 90º and the thigh is parallel to the ground. It is important that the back knee (right) does not touch the ground, this ensures that the muscles are in tension throughout the exercise.

3. Take off with your lead leg (left) and move your back leg (right) forward to move forward and take another stride. Keep your back straight and your abdomen contracted throughout the exercise.

4. Standing between each stride serves as a short break and can help you get more reps.

5. You should feel the involvement only in the quads and glutes. If you start to notice pain in your back, check your technique in front of the gym mirror because you may be leaning too far forward.

PULL THROUGH

The Pull Through is surely one of the most beneficial exercises you can perform to develop your glutes and hamstrings that you are probably not doing.

They generate a unique training stimulus through which you will be able to develop all the muscles of the posterior chain (cervical spinal, thoracic, lumbar, gluteal, hamstring, calf, soleus and flexors of the sole of the foot) with less risk of injury to your spine. vertebral.

Technique

With your back to a cable machine, stand with your feet wider than hip width apart.

HOLD THE CABLE

In front of your hips with the cable that travels through your legs.

USE YOUR WAIST

Feel your hips back until your torso is at a 45-degree angle.

EXTENDS THE HIPS

Explosively extend your hips to push your glutes hard back to the starting position.

Glute bridge

The glute bridge (or glute bridge, for its name in English) is an exercise that works the glutes and the back of the legs; it also helps to strengthen all the muscles of the trunk. Although no machine is needed to do it, it is a very effective exercise and especially suitable for beginners as it is very easy to perform. You can do it at home using a mat or at the gym if you prefer. After just a couple of repetitions, you will notice that your muscles are well activated. If you are looking for an exercise that makes you sweat, feel free to give it a try.

Like squats, the glute bridge exercise works to train the back of the legs and the glutes. Specifically, they work:

• the biceps femoris muscle,
• the semitendinosus muscle,
• the gluteus maximus muscle.

In addition, this exercise is of the compound type, so doing it trains other muscle groups. Specifically, the muscles of the trunk, abdomen and calves are trained.

1.- Initial position

Lie on your back with your back fully against the mat. With your knees bent, place your feet at hip height so that your calves are perpendicular to the floor. The head remains glued to the mat, the view remains towards the ceiling. The neck is an extension of the spinal column. The arms, on both sides of the body with the palms of the hands facing the ground.

2.- Up

Lift your hips off the floor making sure your back, buttocks, and thighs are in a straight line. To fully train your erector spinae muscle, lift your shoulder blades slightly. The knees should not touch when doing the movement, but they should not be too far apart; it is best if you leave a space about the width of a fist between them. Make sure you push your pelvis up using your leg muscles, not your arms.

3.- Down

Hold the position for a second. Then lower your pelvis back down until you almost touch the floor with your butt, but don't touch it (very important!). Once in that position, lift yourself up again. Pay special attention that the glutes are always contracted. To avoid arching or bending your back, you should do the same with the muscles of the abdomen.

4.- repetition

Take a short pause after doing several reps. Do you think you can make it a little more difficult for yourself? Take hold of a peso. The execution is exactly the same, all you have to do is place the weight in question on the abdomen or on the hips and grasp it with your hands.

Step-up or Upload to drawer

The step-up is a unilateral exercise with which we will work our quadriceps, hamstrings, hip flexors and calves. The gluteus maximus and the core muscles or deep muscles of the abdomen also collaborate in this exercise.

We will stand in front of our drawer, bench or chair, with the legs open to the width of the hip and the arms stretched out on both sides of the body (in the case that we do the unloaded version of the exercise, the simplest) . Ideally, the height of the drawer is approximately the same as that of our knee.

We raise our right leg and support it on the top of the drawer, chair or bench and, keeping our back as upright as possible (and that is where our core muscles come into play) we push our right foot on the drawer to push ourselves to upload. We raise both legs and go down with the right leg first.

As it is a unilateral exercise, we will have to repeat it by raising the left leg first. We can alternate one leg and the other each time to achieve a balanced work. Once we have it mastered, we can add more intensity to the exercise by adding load.

LEG EXTENSIONS: Technique and muscles involved

The Leg Extension is an isolation exercise whose target muscle is the training of the quadriceps of the leg.

The leg extension machine has come under heavy attack in the fitness industry for the past two decades. It is accused of creating chronic inflammation of the knee by creating highly compressive forces on the patellofemoral joint, resulting in joint injury.

The reality is that while there is some risk involved in doing this exercise, leg extension is also responsible for helping to build some of the most impressive quads. Additionally, it remains a staple in many programs because it produces results for those who desire muscle hypertrophy.

If you have pain or discomfort, consider some details

☐ Use this exercise only to congest or pump to the end of your routine

☐ Don't use a lot of weight, try to do more repetitions in the series.

☐ Do not use it with high frequency, I recommend once a week

☐ If it hurts, replace the exercise with another, as there are many other alternatives.

TECHNIQUE

To begin the machine leg extension exercise, we must sit on the specific machine for this purpose and place the feet under the padded pads or rollers, so that the knees are aligned with the joint of the machine.

We place our hands gripping the seat or the arms of the chair to stabilize the trunk and we sit in such a way that the back and hips are perfectly supported on the back of the machine. Previously we must load the machine with the chosen weight and once in this position, we must inspire and perform a knee extension in order to lift the weight with the legs until they are horizontal and parallel to the floor, the torso must remain immobile and upright.

We exhale at the end of the movement and begin a slow, controlled descent. The legs must remain parallel to each other throughout the course.

FEMORAL OR ISCHIOTIBIAL CURL: Technique and muscles involved

Lying leg curls or curls work the hamstring muscles, mainly the leg flexors (biceps femoris, semitendinosus, and semimembranosus). This type of exercise also works muscles such as the gluteus maximus and minor, in addition to the calves. Doing a lying leg curl improves the strength you can have in the area.

The lying femoral curl is a type of isolation weight training whose target muscle is the training of the leg femoris.

Technique

We place ourselves in the specific machine for its realization, lying face down with the ankles just under the cushions and the hands holding the grips that are under the support bench. Previously, we load the machine with the weight we want and begin by inhaling while bending the knees to raise the loaded weight with the ankles.

When the knee is bent and the heels are close to the buttocks and we begin to return to the starting position controlling the movement.

STANDING AND SITTING HEEL LIFTS

FOOT HEEL LIFTS

To start with this calf exercise we must place ourselves on the machine putting our shoulders under the padding of it. The toes are placed forward on the platform so that the heels of the foot are free to perform the free movement from top to bottom. The legs should be kept straight so that the feet, hips and shoulders are aligned. Lower your heels at a moderate speed until you feel the work of the Achilles Heel and calves.

SITTING HEEL LIFTS

This exercise is similar to standing calf raises, but now on a machine to sit and support the legs. Position yourself correctly on the heel lift machine by centering your body on the seat and keeping your torso upright. Like the previous exercise, the toes should go on the platform to give the heels free movement. Take a breath as you bring your heels up to their final position, then lower your heels until they are below the instep. Remember to hold for 2-3 seconds contracting your calves as you raise them.

Tips for huge buttocks

1.-One of the most important points to take advantage of is that you start working exercises in which we obtain a peak of activation with zero degrees of hip flexion, that is, in which the exercise achieves maximum activation at the gluteal level, when the hip is in a neutral position. Staying in a neutral position and going further would be extension.

We are going to work with activation peaks at 0 degrees of hip flexion, exercises that have this component as the main part, such as the hip thrust, gluteal bridge, all these exercises where the point that costs the most is precisely in the final part of the route, this part is super important to reach.

2.-The next point, which also has to complement perfectly with what I am commenting on, is that we have to look for exercises where the knee is also in flexion, for example, I have mentioned before the Hip thrust or the gluteal bridge, they are exercises where in addition to working with the hip in extension at 0 degrees of flexion at the point that is most difficult, it has another peculiarity and that is that the knee is flexed. Why is it important that these exercises keep the knee flexed? basically due to active insufficiency at the hamstring level.

What we are looking for is that, with the knee flexion, the hamstring does not work as much and it is the gluteus that really participates actively, as a main engine of all this movement, that is, if we did this same exercise with the knee extended, with the leg extended the gluteus would participate less and it would be the hamstrings that would get much more work.

When we reflect the knee and do exercises such as the gluteal bridge, the hip thrust, etc. What I get precisely is more participation of the gluteus, therefore, these exercises are spectacular when these two things are combined, as I mentioned, the main trigger point or the area that is most difficult to be with the hips in a neutral position. That is, precisely the final part of the gluteal bridge or the eastern hip thrust. With the knee flexed, because this is precisely how we take work off the hamstrings and put work on the buttocks in quotes.

3.-A point that we must take into account when working with abduction exercises, that is, separation of the leg and external rotation of the hip, can be worked with specific, concrete exercises that allow abduction and external rotation, such as, for example, a lateral step, a monster walk, etc. or we can incorporate these two gestures of abduction and external rotation precisely to the work of the aforementioned, such as the gluteal bridge and the hip thrust etc.

4.- The next point would be to work directly taking advantage of the retro version of the pelvis, we have to understand that when we do this gesture, we pull the buttock out, squeeze the abdomen, the buttock and put the hips in, this is a gesture of pelvic retroversion.

The buttocks will be mainly involved in this retroversion gesture, this means that, mainly when you make a gesture in which the maximum activation will be at this neutral hip point, you have to look for pelvic retroversion, tighten the abdomen and tighten the gluteus, this will strengthen the gluteus much more.

Does this mean that we have to take advantage of pelvic retroversion in all exercises? not in all, for example, it is very common that when we go to the gym we observe how when a person squats in the final part, makes that gesture of your pelvic version, there it is not necessary, because the gluteal activation peak in the squat It does not occur with the neutral hip, it occurs precisely in the lower part, when the gluteus is in elongation, but we will comment on this later, because it is interesting too.

5.- It is important that we work high loads first, with some exercises that involve performing with high loads, such as the squat or deadlift, which are exercises that are mainly to move kilos and medium loads, of course also exercises that involve move less cargo, but involve more congestion. For example, working with elastic bands, monster walk, side steps, etc.

Working with high loads, medium loads and low loads, would be a quite ideal point, for example, we can work with high loads, squats, deadlifts, hip thrust or glute bridge. We can work with medium loads such as extensions on the bench to make hyper extensions and we work with low loads for those that involve more congestion, with this wide and combination of loads, it will be a very interesting job.

6.- It would imply working directly with three types of stimulus, the first stimulus that enhances the buttocks, elongation, that is, the maximum activation peak is achieved in elongation, as, for example, we can achieve it with the squat and with the weight dead where you notice mainly the gluteus, which is what is going to be linked to those soreness, with that pain, with that damage to the gluteus. This occurs in the lowest part of the route where the gluteus is most activated. For example, in a squat, it is when the gluteus is elongated and we are in the lowest part, so the lower we go, the longer it takes us to activate this gluteus. We will combine exercises where we enhance

the gluteus in elongation. In stretching we would take exercises as we have already mentioned before, where we would mainly work the gluteus in shortening where, they receive maximum contraction with the hip being at 0 degrees, such as a hip thrust, a gluteal bridge, etc.

We will also work with congestion exercises, for example, doing hip abductions with the monster walk and doing hip raises also on the floor, all those exercises that we seek at the end of congestion, we seek to work more repetitions and we seek to work mainly on the gluteus. quite congested.

You see that we have commented before and we have put these exercises, the exercises in which we achieve maximum glute activation at zero degrees of hip extension and we have put them in a separate point from the one I just mentioned. In itself, I have told you that there are three main stimuli of elongation, contraction and in addition to congestion.

The gluteal bridge or the hip thrust are the exercises that will be most linked to this glute activation, these will be the exercises in which the force vector is horizontal, that is, in which we push from the back to the front as best as possible. be this gluteal bridge or this hip thrust, in fact when we compare for example glute activation in exercises such as squats, strides or deadlifts and we compare it with a hip thrust or with a gluteal bridge, we see that these activate more the gluteus.

Although of course, as I have already mentioned, the perfect thing would be to combine it with the previous ones, recapitulating what I would advise you, I would advise you to work with exercises such as the hip thrust or the gluteal bridge in which the maximum activation occurs with the hip in neutral and also, we would work with this retroversion of the pelvis, which would be to force that gesture a little more, to tighten the gluteus more.

You ask yourself, it has not been clear to me about pelvic retroversion, what does it consist of? as if you wanted to squeeze the gluteus as much as possible, it would be a similar gesture, but while doing the exercise. We have said that it is super important to work mainly on these exercises with the knee flexed, because we take the hamstrings out of the equation a little and we get more gains.

We have also said that it must be combined with other movement patterns, such as hip abduction, that is, this hip separation and external rotation, in fact, you can perfectly do that gluteal bridge or hip thrust exercise and work in abduction and external rotation, to further enhance.

Of course, we have also commented that you have to work with different types of exercises and with different types of loads, stimuli, for example: exercises with maximum elongation, exercises where we seek that maximum contraction and congestion exercises. That will also be totally linked to the type of load that will be used, for example, in a squat we will work with higher loads, with a lot of elongation and it will be more linked to muscle damage in exercises where we are looking the maximum contraction at the end, such as a glute bridge or a hip thrust, the loads are going to be high. And finally, the congestion exercises, it is important that we work it with more repetitions in a much broader spectrum, but seeking to focus more on the gluteus.

Why aren't your legs growing?

First of all, let's analyze what is the most common problem faced by people who do not develop their legs as they would like. From there, I will give some practical advice. We will start with frequency, one of the most common problems for which people have problems when training their legs.

Many of the people who start training in a gym, start with a divided routine, also known as Weider routines frequency 1, although fortunately this has changed over time, some trainers and many people still recommend this routine, although it can be To achieve good results, it is not the best option, nor the most optimal, since there may be muscular imbalances as in the case of the legs.

This type of routine cannot give all the potential we have, due to the frequency of training, this type of routine usually trains a muscle group per day, for example, on Monday the pectorals, on Tuesday the back, on Wednesday the shoulders, the Thursday the biceps and triceps, Friday the legs or in any other order but the same pattern is always repeated, one muscle group per day and so that we can see the great imbalance that there may be, because you are training the upper part of your body and legs only one day. The weider frequency 2 routine makes a lot more sense.

However, there are also some women who give more priority and much frequency to the legs and train them several times a week, however, they do not have the desired results since they are not giving the adequate stimulus or they are not getting enough rest.

Obviously for men and women it is the same advice, first of all choose the best exercises to develop the legs, I name some in the following list, for example, the squat and all its variants, Bulgarian squat and front squat etc.

On the other hand, there would be Hip thrust, deadlift and its variants, quadriceps extensions, of course the press and heel raises.

Of course there are other exercises with which we can vary, but at least include these exercises in your leg routine. In the leg routine you have to train the buttocks, for example, the gluteus maximus is the largest muscle that the human body has and it makes no sense not to train it, in fact, I cannot imagine large legs and a small buttock, it does not have sense, in addition to that if we strengthen the buttocks we will have stronger legs.

For example, the squat and the deadlift will be greatly improved, if we work the glutes in an isolated way, a perfect exercise for this is the Hip thrust.

Once we have the exercises that are going to give us the best results, we would move on to the second advice, which is the execution of each of them to develop strength and hypertrophy, it is necessary to do the correct range and route. Always, for most exercises we have to perform a full range of travel, because the gains are going to be greater. To give an example, in the squat, the deeper we go down, the more muscle fibers will be involved, which will give us greater long-term gains and this happens with the same with any other type of exercise, the more range we travel. more muscle fibers we are going to involve. A very common mistake that I usually see in gyms is with the strides and the squat, the strides must be lowered as much as possible and that the knee is close to the ground and when climbing does not support the hands against the legs, because we are helping each other and remember that it is a leg workout.

The frequency

As we mentioned at the beginning if we want to develop sufficiently large and strong legs, we should train them at least twice a week and even three times, but with twice would be the correct frequency, for that we could do a full body routine or a routine torso-leg, pull-push, weider frequency 2, and so on. But that your routine is at least twice the leg a week.

Progression over time

If you want to increase muscle mass, it is not enough to go to the gym, you have to go to the gym to train and go with the mentality of progressing, lifting more weight or training more intensely than the previous training and so on. If you are training in the gym and you have been lifting the same weight for more than a month and continue to lift the same weight, with the same repetitions, the same number of rest times, it is most likely that you will not have an increase in muscle mass in your legs, nor in any other muscle group and especially if you are a beginner, since when you are beginners you can improve much faster.

We are not talking about raising weight to the bar without meaning, the smart thing is to keep track of the weight you put on the bar, the weight of the dumbbells, your marks and that at the end of the week or the month, you know that you raised , even if it is a kilo in your marks. Remember, everything must be measurable, because you must know your progress.

Remember that for a muscle to grow we must give them reasons to grow and this applies with mechanical stress and metabolic stress, basically training heavy. Taking this factor into account, we must increase the loads over time and as a consequence also increase the size of the legs.

The perception of failure

When was the last time you went to failure doing a bicep curl or for example doing chin-ups or bench press, surely that feeling will be familiar to you, but I wonder, when was the last time you reached muscle failure in squat or weight? dead. Something that I would like to make clear is that the sensation of failure in the legs is not going to be the same as in the arms, the legs hold much more than the arms and as you know many people do not reach the failure of the squat and it is not That he is recommending you to get there, however, to know where the fault is, to know where the limit is, you have to cross it from time to time.

I remember one time I was deadlifting, a five-by-five (strength) routine and I swore I was doing five reps with that weight and I was doing the last rep and a gym trainer came in and was with someone else and said to the guy This is how you do a deadlift, and I was motivated because I was taking an example, I did another and another and another repetition and I did about 9 repetitions and I swore that I did 5 and it was simply like that perception I had of the failure, because I swore I was going to reach failure in 5 reps. From there I began to rethink leg training and the same has happened with people with whom I have trained in the gym, who believe that a limit is already close but there is still a long way to go to reach that limit.

So, as I said before, to know where the limit is, you have to cross it from time to time, however this point could be debatable.

Having adequate food and rest is very important, if you have thin legs and are thin in general and it is difficult for you to increase muscle mass and you feel that you are giving everything in training and you do not increase body weight and do not increase the loads in the exercises that you are doing, you should review your diet and your rest well.

Gluteal routine example

Leg and gluteal work should be at least 2 times a week, ie a frequency of at least 2 times a week, being a large muscle, the series should be in a range of 12 to 24 series per week. As for repetitions, being a muscle with equal fast and slow fibers, you should combine low and high repetitions in your training.

All this will depend on the training time you dedicate to the glutes, if you combine it on the same day with leg or hamstrings, or separately. Of course also if you are going to do strength or hypertrophy training or a hybrid or mixed training on the same day of strength and hypertrophy. There are a range of possibilities.

An example of a glute routine without considering the work of quadriceps and hamstrings, it can look like this.

EXERCISE	SERIES	REP.
SUMO SQUAT	4	8
HIP-THRUST	4	6
PULL-THROUGH	3	10
HIP-THRUST	4	12
GLUTE BRIDGE	3	20

Leg routine example

Hypertrophy and Strength

Leg routine example

Day A

EXERCISE	SET	REPETITION
SQUAT		4 X 10
deadlift exercise sumo		4 X 10
Hip Thrust		4 X 10
Romanian Deadlift		3 X 10
machine extensions		4 x 15
Standing Heel Raises		5 x 12

Day B

EXERCISE	SET	REPETITION
SQUAT		4 X 6
Conventional deadlift		4 X 6
Hip Thrust		4 X 8
femoral curl (hamstrings)		3 X12
machine extensions		4 x 15
Standing Heel Raises		5 x 12

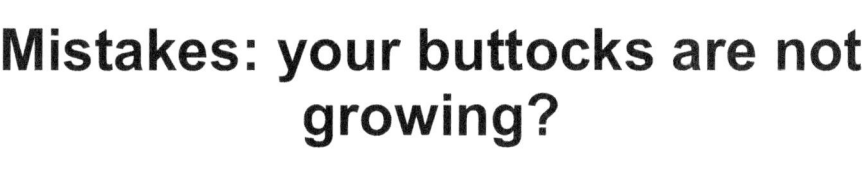

Mistakes: your buttocks are not growing?

1.- Improve your stress and your quality of sleep. We all know that stress is something we deal with today and can often affect the hormonal environment.

2.- Increase the frequency of training, it may be that you are doing little. Review your routine.

3.- Choose exercises that you notice work, normally people do not leave our comfort zone

4.- Eat according to your goals. Check your daily macronutrients.

5.- Discipline is the key, you have to be constant and progress.

6.- You have to train heavy, the muscle needs stimulation. Nobody grows without effort.

7.- Quality of exercises is better than quantity of exercises. You may be overdoing it. Review your routine.

Time is the most precious thing we have, for the same reason I thank you for taking the time to read the book, I hope it helps you to enhance your performance and obtain better results in your training.

Author

Self-taught, passionate about nutrition, metabolism, fitness in general and fasting, he studied chemical engineering. I am from Veracruz, Mexico. Always updating myself, based on science studies, meta-analysis and research. Always trying to help people who want to take control of their health.

Contact

Comments, doubts, constructive criticism or for contact by WhatsApp send message to:

ing_isr@hotmail.com

If you like these themes, I offer you one of the titles in the list below for free (pdf).

Message with the title of the book you want

ing_isr@hotmail.com

Book author

- Scientific Weight Training
- Stress: Tools to Reduce and Eliminate It
- Intermittent fasting in sport
- ENERGY ALL DAY
- 10 Anti-Aging Habits
- How to be smarter
- 15 METHODS TO LOSE WEIGHT
- MEGA BUTTOCKS
- TESTOSTERONE: Raise Your Level Naturally
- Ketogenic Diet in Sports
- The real pandemic
- Intermittent fasting and ketogenic diet in sport

MEGA BUTTOCKS AND LEGS

Scientific Buttocks and Legs Training

Iván Salinas Román

Printed in Great Britain
by Amazon

10522114R00092